Trouble at Catskill Creek

A. G. GERSDORF

Fearon Education
a division of
DAVID S. LAKE PUBLISHERS
Belmont, California

The PACEMAKER BESTELLERS

Bestellers I

Diamonds in the Dirt
Night of the Kachina
The Verlaine Crossing
Silvabamba
The Money Game
Flight to Fear
The Time Trap
The Candy Man
Three Mile House
Dream of the Dead

Bestellers II

Black Beach
Crash Dive
Wind Over Stonehenge
Gypsy
Escape from Tomorrow
The Demeter Star
North to Oak Island
So Wild a Dream
Wet Fire
Tiger, Lion, Hawk

Bestellers III

Star Gold
Bad Moon
Jungle Jenny
Secret Spy
Little Big Top
The Animals
Counterfeit!
Night of Fire and Blood
Village of Vampires
I Died Here

Bestellers IV

Dares
Welcome to Skull Canyon
Blackbeard's Medal
Time's Reach
Trouble at Catskill Creek
The Cardiff Hill Mystery
Tomorrow's Child
Hong Kong Heat
Follow the Whales
A Changed Man

Cover and interior illustrator: Nanette Biers

Copyright © 1988 by David S. Lake Publishers, 19 Davis Drive, Belmont, CA 94002. All rights reserved. No part of this book may be reproduced by any means, transmitted, or translated into a machine language without written permission from the publisher.

ISBN 0-8224-5339-8

Library of Congress Catalog Card Number: 87-80129

Printed in the United States of America

1. 9 8 7 6 5 4 3 2 1

CONTENTS

- **1** THE NEW LAKE 1
- **2** GRANDPA AND HIS GEESE 6
- **3** THE GRAVEYARDS 15
- **4** GHOSTS! 20
- **5** CHANGES 25
- **6** THE BREAK-IN 32
- **7** MOVING DAY 38
- **8** FIRE! 46
- **9** ANSWERS AT LAST 51
- **10** CROFT LAKE 58

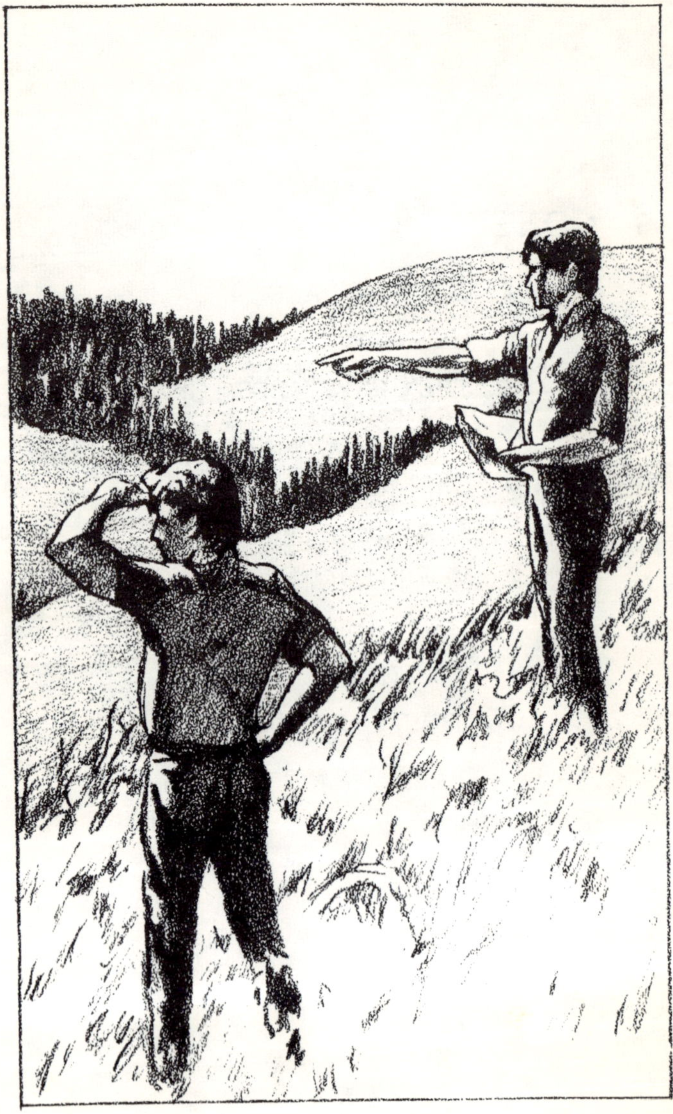

CHAPTER **1**
THE NEW LAKE

"Here," I said, pointing to the ground. "This is where you'll build Grandpa's house."

Rip Turner and I stood together in a wide field on a hillside. Goldy, Rip's collie, ran in circles through the tall grass. His long tail stirred up tiny butterflies.

All around us the Catskill Mountains rose toward the sky. They looked dark blue in the morning light. Spring had come at last. The trees wore bright green leaves. Robins flew overhead. It was going to be a great Saturday.

Rip looked up the hill. "Old Charlie will hate it, you know."

Charlie Croft is my grandfather. He often told me I was wasting time and money on the new house. "I won't move there. I have a house already," he'd say.

Grandpa lived in the valley, in the little town of Snowfall. He was born there, as were his parents, grandparents, and children. Snowfall was filled with Crofts.

I showed Rip a drawing. "This is what the new house will look like. Here's the fireplace, and there's the porch. Grandpa will be able to see the whole lake."

Rip smiled. "He hates the lake, and it's not even built yet."

"He'll get used to it. We all will."

I moved off toward the woods, and Rip followed. "This is where we'll dig the goose pond," I said.

"Those silly geese. Old Charlie seems to think they're real people."

Rip was right. Grandpa had often said, "My geese are my family." Not everyone liked Grandpa's geese. They made a lot of noise. Often they got out of the yard and hissed at people in town.

"If we don't move the geese," I said, "we won't be able to move Grandpa."

Rip pulled a notebook and pen from his pocket. "What about these trees?"

Some of the trees were more than six stories tall. "You'll have to cut a few," I said. "But don't cut too many. They'll help keep the snow away from the house when winter comes."

A nearby stream bubbled down the mountain. Goldy drank from the ice-cold water. I said, "We'll block off part of this stream and send it to the pond. That way the geese will have fresh water."

Rip nodded and wrote in his notebook. Rip Turner is my wife's brother. He can build almost anything, even a goose pond.

I waited while Rip and Goldy walked around the field. Rip stopped now and then to take notes. Goldy grew tired and lay down under a bush to rest.

I sat on the hillside with my back to the mountain. Below me was the old stone house where Karen and I lived. Smoke floated out its chimney. The days were warm now, but the nights still held the cold.

I wasn't born in Snowfall. My father left the valley when he was 20 years old. He went to New York and married a city woman. I grew up on busy streets and in crowded rooms. But each summer I went to the Catskills. I always loved the mountains.

When high school was at last behind me, I moved to Snowfall and lived with Grandpa. Later I met Karen Ann Turner, and we got married. We bought the old stone house near the town of Dutch Center. For two years we'd been fixing it up.

Dutch Center was on Acorn Road. The town had been made up of a few stores, one bank, and two schools. Acorn Road ran down to Snowfall, six miles away. It passed our place on its way to the valley and Grandpa's house.

Acorn Road was once a quiet road. Now trucks shook the ground all day long.

People from New York City were coming to build a lake. They planned to cut off Catskill Creek. Its waters would then fill the valley.

Catskill Creek was a rocky river. It passed behind Snowfall and Grandpa's house. Tourists came every summer to ride its white rushing waters.

Before the river could become a lake, the valley had to be cleared. All the trees, buildings, and people had to go.

No one in the valley wanted the lake. People put up a good fight against it. But they lost. Everyone in Snowfall had to sell their land to the City of New York. Now they were looking for new homes on higher ground. Grandpa would live by us, in the house Rip would build.

The lake would take three years to finish. Hundreds of workers and their families had come to the mountains. New houses were built for them in Dutch Center. When the lake was done, many of the workers would go back to New York. But some would stay. The Catskills can make people want to do that.

My train of thought was broken by the sound of a slamming door. Karen stood on the back steps of our house, waving her arms in the air.

"Come quickly, Will!" she cried. Goldy barked and raced toward her. I jumped to my feet and ran after him.

"What is it, Karen?"

"We just got a telephone call from the police in Snowfall. Old Charlie is on the warpath again!"

CHAPTER 2
GRANDPA AND HIS GEESE

Rip laughed when he heard about Grandpa. "There's no need for bulldozers there. Old Charlie will tear down Snowfall all by himself."

Rip climbed into his pickup truck, and Goldy jumped in back. I helped my wife into her seat. Our baby wasn't due for three months, but Karen was getting very large. "We mountain girls have big babies," she'd said.

Rip drove fast along Acorn Road into Snowfall. We didn't have to look far to find Grandpa. He stood in the middle of the road in front of his house. He was shouting as loud as he could. In one hand he shook a big stick. In the other he held a sheet of paper.

Rip pulled over and we got out.

"Grandpa!" I called, running up to him.

"Don't try to stop me, Will. I'm going to get one of those city boys. Then maybe they'll go away and leave me in peace."

"They're not going anywhere, Grandpa. They have a job to do here."

"Some job," he said. "Look at this, just look!" He handed me the paper.

The letter said Grandpa had to move out of Snowfall.

"You already know you have to move," I said. "They're building a *lake* here. You can't live under water! Most of your neighbors have already left."

"I'm not leaving Snowfall, Will. This is my home." He opened the gate to his yard and walked toward the house.

"He doesn't even own this place anymore," I said to Karen.

"Let him be. He's a sad old man."

Just then some children ran by.

"Where are you going?" Rip called to them.

One boy slowed down. "They're moving the Davis house!"

Goldy ran after them. Rip turned to us. "Let's take a look."

Karen and I followed at a walk. The Davis family lived in a stone house that was more than two hundred years old. They'd sold their land but wanted to keep the house.

8 *Trouble at Catskill Creek*

Last week, strong jacks on all sides of the house had been used to lift it off the ground. Workers then built a log platform under it. They put wheels on the platform. Today a tractor was taking the house out of the valley.

The tractor moved very, very slowly. It would need a whole day to reach Dutch Center. Land there had been made ready for the house. Tomorrow the tractor would come back to Snowfall for another house.

Karen and I walked back to Grandpa's. She said, "It's too bad Old Charlie's house can't be moved."

"I'm afraid it's not strong enough. They'll just tear it down when he leaves."

A well-worn path led us behind the house.

"Look at that!" Karen whispered.

Grandpa sat in his rocking chair in the middle of the yard. All around him were dozens of large white geese picking at the ground and each other. Grandpa was talking to one of them.

"Can you believe it, Martha? Those city men are moving your house. They're dragging it halfway up the mountain. You would cry your eyes out if you saw it."

Karen asked me softly, "Which goose is Martha?"

"I don't know. They all look the same to me."

One of those birds was called Martha Croft Davis. Grandpa had named each goose after someone in our family. The real Martha Croft Davis was Grandpa's aunt. She had died before I was born. She and her husband used to live in the Davis house.

George Croft was Grandpa's brother. He died long ago. Grandpa likes to think his brother can still hear him.

Grandpa always had company.

Karen covered her mouth and laughed out loud. "He looks like he's floating in a sea of white feathers."

Grandpa didn't hear her. But the geese did. All at once they started honking and hissing. Then they opened their big wings and ran straight at us.

Karen and I shouted, stamped the ground, and clapped our hands. The geese ran around us in circles, still honking.

"Hello, Will. Hello, Karen." Grandpa moved toward us through all the birds. He no longer seemed so angry. "How's the baby?"

Karen touched her stomach. "Big as a horse, and just as strong."

"Glad to hear it. Come on inside."

We followed him through the back door. The kitchen smelled of coffee and bacon. The breakfast dishes were already washed and put away. Grandpa poured coffee into cups. We carried them to the front porch and sat together on a wide swing.

"How are the geese?" I asked.

He shook his head. "They're not as stupid as people think. They see the changes in the valley. And let me tell you, they don't like them."

"What's done is done, Grandpa. The new lake will store clean water for people in New York. You know they can't drink out of the ocean. Our water's the best in the world. We have to share it."

"They have no business building a lake on top of my home." Grandpa pulled a pipe out of his pocket but didn't light it. His doctor wouldn't let him smoke. He put the empty pipe in his mouth.

Karen said, "You were paid for your house. They didn't take it."

He frowned. "They paid me, yes. But Crofts have lived in this valley since Indian days. Now a lot of strangers want to fill it with water."

"Here come some of those strangers now," I said. A green New York City jeep was moving down Acorn Road. Lately green jeeps were everywhere. This one was driven by Robert Adler, head of the lake project. He and his wife lived in the Hanson house. Last Christmas the Hansons had moved to California.

12 *Trouble at Catskill Creek*

The jeep stopped in front of Grandpa's house. Mr. Adler, his wife, and two men climbed out. The men wore heavy green work clothes. Mrs. Adler wore a pink dress and high-heeled shoes. She had a hard time walking on the dirt path.

Mr. Adler said hello. Grandpa turned away, the pipe between his teeth.

Adler said to me, "I'd like you to meet my wife, Darlene." She was a tall, thin woman who was wearing a lot of makeup. A smile crossed her face, but she didn't look happy. She looked as if she'd rather be on the moon.

"And have you met my right-hand men? These are the Brown brothers, Mark and Pete. They're helping me pull down Snowfall."

Both men were short and looked strong. Their skin was dark from working in the sun. "Nice to know you," they said to us.

Grandpa suddenly pushed himself off the swing and walked into the house. I knew he'd be going out back to talk to his geese.

I started to speak, but Mr. Adler cut in. "Don't worry about your grandfather, Will. Everyone in town wants us to go away. I can't say I blame them much. That's why we're meeting as many people as we can. We want to show them we're not so bad."

"Give them time," Karen said. "They'll come around. Would you like to sit down?"

I held up my cup. "There's lots of coffee."

"No, thank you," said Mr. Adler. "We've got work to do. My people are still pulling up the railroads. And Monday we start digging up the graveyards."

Just then a wave of white feathers raced around the corner of the house. A big hissing goose attacked the visitors with its mouth wide open. Mrs. Adler screamed and nearly fell off her shoes. Her husband tried to scare away the goose, but he wasn't fast enough. The bird chased Mrs. Adler down the path and into the road.

The men quickly followed. The goose honked at the jeep as it drove away.

"Grandpa!" I shouted.

When he stepped out from around the corner, Grandpa was trying not to grin. He put the pipe in his mouth and his hands in his pockets. "Is something the matter, Will?"

I spoke with a hard voice. "You set that goose on them, didn't you?"

Grandpa smiled sweetly. Karen was laughing. "Martha doesn't take to strangers," Grandpa said. "It's as simple as that."

So it was that big mean goose that was Martha Croft Davis. She waddled over to a flowering bush and sat down to clean her feathers.

Grandpa closed the gate and gazed down the road. "They were lucky. I should have met them with something more than a mad bird."

"You're talking through your hat," said Karen. "You wouldn't hurt a mouse."

"I don't know," Grandpa answered. "Even a mouse might bite you if you took away its home." He walked off toward the back of the house.

Karen frowned. "Old Charlie's up to something."

"Could be," I said. "I think he'd *like* to get himself in trouble."

That night, while Darlene Adler was reading in bed, the Hanson house caught fire. Darlene woke her husband and they escaped, but some of their things burned up.

I wasn't the only one who thought Grandpa might have finally found his trouble.

CHAPTER **3**
THE GRAVEYARDS

There were seven graveyards in the valley, with more than 800 graves. Some of the headstones were so old the names had worn off. All the graves were to be moved to higher ground. On Sunday, flowers were put on each of them. Then the churches held special services.

Many of the graves belonged to members of the Croft family. Grandpa knew them all. He told us about cousins, great-aunts, and great-great-grandmothers.

"Here's the grave of my great-uncle Clement Croft." Grandpa said. "He once drank too much and took his neighbor's horse. The people of Snowfall wanted to hang him. But he kept saying the horse took *him*. He said they should hang the horse. In the end they sent him home to sleep it off."

We spent the whole day among the graves. Grandpa wouldn't talk about the lake or the Hanson fire. He was happy living in the past.

The next day, Adler's workers started digging up and moving the graves. It would be a month before they'd finish. I wondered if the Crofts would be kept together. Maybe nobody cared except Grandpa.

That Monday, as always, I went to work at the Dutch Center Post Office. A while back, I'd been sorting mail for 500 families. Now I sorted for 2,000. Mr. Sanders was once the only mailman. Now there were four.

In Dutch Center, there were more new homes than old ones. Most of the people from the valley were moving here. New stores popped up almost overnight. New roads were cut through the forests. Two banks and a big school went up. Dutch Center turned into a small city right before our eyes.

The Adlers moved to a new place in Dutch Center. They stopped by the post office to rent a box for their mail.

"I suppose you heard about the fire," Mr. Adler said to me.

"Everyone's talking about it. We're glad you're both safe."

"I think someone wanted to hurt us."

It was easy to see who Adler thought that someone might be.

"My grandfather didn't do it," I said. "People think he's a little strange. I know that. But put yourself in his shoes. How do you think you'd feel if your town was being torn down?"

"Perhaps you're right. But see my side of it. I'm worried about my wife and my workers."

"There are lots of people as angry as Grandpa. Anyone could have started that fire."

That's what I believed, anyway. Yet all day long the people of Dutch Center were nice to me—almost too nice. No one said out loud that Grandpa had done it. But their eyes seemed to be saying, "You're such a nice young man. It's too bad about your grandfather."

Grandpa's friends in Snowfall knew better. Many of them were cousins, and cousins of cousins. Everyone liked Old Charlie.

I was glad when five o'clock came and I could go home. Karen sat at the kitchen table with an open book in her hands. "How about Ronald?" she asked when I walked in.

"Ronald who?" Then I saw that the book was *Names for Baby*.

"Do you like the *name* Ronald?" she said.

I pulled out a chair and sat across from her. "We can't use Ronald. That's one of the geese, named after my great-grandfather."

"How about Daniel?"

"Second cousin. In fact, I think two of the geese are called Daniel."

"Martin?"

"Grandma's brother."

"This is silly, Will."

"Maybe we'll have a girl. Most of the Crofts were men. It'd be simpler to find a girl's name that's not in the family."

We talked about names all through dinner. Finally we gave up on finding one that hadn't been used on a goose.

"I have an idea," Karen said just before the telephone rang. "We'll call this baby Number One. The next one can be Number Two."

I laughed and answered the phone.

"Will? This is Robert Adler."

"What can I do for you?"

He sounded worried. "Last night we had the fire. Tonight we have a new problem."

After I hung up, Karen asked me what was wrong. "You look surprised," she said.

I reached for my boots. "You're not going to believe this. Four people in Snowfall called the police tonight. They all said they saw ghosts in town."

"Ghosts?"

CHAPTER 4
GHOSTS!

A silver moon was hiding behind the clouds. The branches of trees reached toward the moon like long skinny fingers. I locked my car doors before starting the engine.

Adler was waiting for me at Grandpa's house. He and Grandpa sat quietly in the living room. Grandpa's hair was messy, and he wore a bathrobe. Mr. Adler rubbed his eyes as I said hello and found a chair.

"What happened?" I asked.

Adler answered with a tired voice. "You know Norma and Buddy Johnson? They told the police tonight they saw ghosts dancing by the river."

"And the police believed them?"

"No. Of course not. Then two more people called to say the same thing—ghosts were dancing on the banks of Catskill Creek."

"What do you care?" I asked. "You're not a policeman. You're here to build a lake."

Adler looked at Grandpa and then back at me. "I'm afraid the people in Snowfall will blame me for the ghosts. The Johnsons say they come from the graveyards we're moving."

"They must be joking," I said. Adler couldn't see Grandpa's face behind the pipe in his hand. I could, however. And I could see that Grandpa was smiling from ear to ear.

Adler shook his head. "I'm not so sure."

"So why did you call me?"

He didn't seem to like the question. "You work at the Dutch Center Post Office. People are going in and out of there all day long. Perhaps you'll hear something that will clear this up."

I didn't believe him. Adler had to have another reason for calling.

Grandpa stood up. "It's late and I'm going back to bed. Good night, Mr. Adler. Good night, Will." He winked at me as he left the room.

Adler moved closer. "Now I can tell you why I came. I think your grandfather might be causing problems for me."

"You came here to make sure he was sleeping, didn't you?" Adler said nothing. I was angry. "I told you before that Grandpa didn't start that fire. And tonight he didn't run around wearing a bed sheet."

"I'm not saying he did, Will. But you should know that my men are watching him. Every time he leaves this house, he'll be followed. When he's sleeping, there'll be someone outside making sure he stays put."

I tried to hold my voice down. "You can't do that. You have no right. My grandfather's not the person you're looking for."

Adler stood up and pulled on his coat. "Maybe he is and maybe he isn't. If anything happens while we're watching him, we'll know he didn't do it. Then we'll leave him alone."

I walked Adler to the door. "I'm going to hold you to that. Old Charlie's my grandfather. If you hurt him, you hurt me. Then your problems are only beginning."

"Lots of people don't like us, Will. You just keep Old Charlie out of my way."

I closed the door and waited until he passed through the gate. "Grandpa!" I called. I knew he wasn't sleeping. No doubt he'd heard every word Adler had said. I found him in the kitchen, heating milk on the stove.

"You listened to us, didn't you?" He grinned. I gently took him by the arm and turned him around. Then I asked him very clearly, "Are you haunting Catskill Creek?"

"No, Will, I'm not. But I can tell you who is. All the Crofts in the graveyards are walking the night. They want the strangers from New York to go home. They want Snowfall to stay as it's been for hundreds of years."

"Ghosts aren't real, and you know it."

He frowned. "Do I, Will? Do any of us know that for sure?"

I knew Grandpa was trying to scare me. It was working, too. I remembered the ghost stories he used to tell when I was a kid. No one told a ghost story better than Old Charlie.

"Please, Grandpa, be careful. You have to be good or you'll get into trouble."

"I'm always good," he said.

Karen was waiting for me at home. I told her about the strange meeting.

She asked, "Do you think your grandfather's playing ghost in Snowfall?"

"He says he's not. I want to believe him. He's never lied to me before."

Later Karen told me Darlene Adler had paid us a visit. "She really misses New York City," Karen said.

"I can tell. She still wears city clothes."

My wife nodded. "I told her not to wear high heels. She should buy a pair of boots. Everyone wears boots here, even the kids. She said she'd die first!"

Karen and I talked for a long time. At last we went to bed. Then I had a dream that set my heart pounding. It got so bad my chest felt as if a train were running through it. I saw myself standing in the dark beside Catskill Creek. All around me danced white shadows. They rose and fell in never-ending waves. I tried to fight them, but they laughed at me. Suddenly they all turned into moving flames. As they burned they danced faster and laughed even louder.

I woke up. The sheets were wet with sweat. In my mind I still saw the flames and heard the mad laughter.

CHAPTER **5**
CHANGES

In June, the Snowfall Post Office finally closed. All the valley's mail was now sent to Dutch Center.

Three old churches were moved from Snowfall to higher ground. Robert Adler gave each one a new bell. The Snowfall school was too old to move. The children cried when it was broken up and trucked away in pieces.

Our son was born at the end of July. He weighed ten pounds. Maybe Karen had been right about mountain women and big babies.

We named our son Charles. That was the only boy's name we liked that some goose didn't have, too. Karen and I wanted to call him Chuck. But from the very first everyone called him Young Charlie.

All summer long Rip and his friends worked on Grandpa's new house. It was beautiful, with a wide porch and a stone fireplace. Later they dug the goose pond.

Now and then during the summer, ghosts were seen dancing near Catskill Creek. They came out only on cloudy nights when the moon was hidden. People were too scared to get close to them.

Adler had other problems, too. Someone poured sugar into a tractor's gas tank. The machine was ruined. Adler sent it back to New York. He was very angry, but he knew Grandpa didn't do it. Mark Brown had been watching Grandpa's house that night. He told Adler that Charlie had never gone out. Grandpa was left alone from then on.

By the time Young Charlie was born, everyone had moved from Snowfall. Everyone, that is, but Grandpa.

Adler didn't waste any more time trying to tell Grandpa to leave. He had too much to do before winter came. Snow fell early in the mountains. It could stop the lake project until next spring. Adler would worry about one crazy old man later.

We thought Grandpa would come with us the day they turned off the power to his house. He didn't.

"I have a wood stove and a fireplace," he said. "And enough logs to last three winters. I'll get by without an icebox. You'll see. I'll do just fine."

As far as we could tell, he did.

The air in the valley became black with the smoke of burning trees. Then bulldozers began clearing the ground. Rocks that were too large to move were blown up.

Workers were building a long low hill all around the land that would become the lake. They pressed the earth down so it was hard as rock. The hillsides would hold the water in the lake like a piecrust. A dam was built to keep the lake from getting too full. When opened, it could send the water into a side stream.

Other workers were laying big pipes into deep holes. Later they would cover the pipes with dirt. This pipeline would go all the way to New York City.

Hundreds of men and women worked together to build the lake. Every day the sounds of saws and big machines set the ground shaking. The valley slowly turned into a land of sand and stones.

A bridge was going in so cars could cross the lake. Concrete was poured into forms to make blocks. Tall cranes lifted the blocks into place. It would be a pretty bridge, everyone said. Everyone except Old Charlie.

Mark and Pete Brown pulled down Snowfall building by building. Grandpa stayed indoors the day they took out the house next to his.

Karen and I talked to him many times about moving.

"Forget it, Will," he always answered. "I'm not leaving Snowfall."

I said, "Mr. Adler has been very kind to let you stay this long. But you've got to get ready to go. Have you packed at all?"

"No."

"Then Karen and I will do it for you."

We went to Grandpa's house every weekend and filled boxes. Grandpa didn't stop us. But he wouldn't let us throw anything away. And he also wouldn't let us take any of the boxes home with us.

One Sunday afternoon I was cleaning out the tool house. There I found a long thin piece of leather. Three smaller pieces were sewn into it in circles at one end. I didn't know what the thing was. When I asked Grandpa, he said, "It's nothing," and took it away from me.

Grandpa wouldn't leave the valley at all that summer. He was almost always around the house. "I don't want Adler tearing it down when I'm not looking," he said.

Karen did Grandpa's shopping in Dutch Center. I brought him his mail. Twice a week we took Young Charlie to visit. Grandpa loved the baby. "He's a Croft all right. Big as a bear and just as strong."

Last September, we were all sitting together before Grandpa's fireplace. There was a knock at the door. "It's not locked," Grandpa called out. "Come on in."

The door slowly opened and Mr. Adler stepped inside. "Hello, everyone." Behind him we could see the Brown brothers. They weren't smiling.

Karen and I looked at each other. Young Charlie was sleeping in her arms. Grandpa waved the men inside.

"Get some coffee, Will," he said.

From the kitchen, I heard them talking about the weather and the lake.

"Here you go," I said, passing cups around. I sat on the floor next to Grandpa's chair.

Adler took a drink before speaking to Grandpa. "Mr. Croft, I should have made you move when your neighbors did. I can't wait any longer."

This was it. I said gently, "The time has come to go, Grandpa. You won't really be leaving Snowfall. Snowfall's already left you. A town with no people and no buildings isn't a town anymore. Snowfall's gone."

Adler added, "You have no telephone. Your heat comes from this fireplace. You're eating out of cans." He waved toward me. "Your grandson here has a house all ready for you. I've seen it. You'll like it very much."

Grandpa looked at the floor. He didn't say anything. I put my hand on his. Even with the fire, his fingers were cold.

"Grandpa," I said.

"I heard you."

Adler finished his coffee and thanked Grandpa. Then he said, "I'd like to see you outside, Will."

Karen frowned. Grandpa looked at the fire and said nothing. I pulled on my coat. The Brown brothers followed us onto the porch.

"Grandpa won't cause any more trouble," I said. "Give me two days to get him moved. Then you can have the house."

"I'm glad to hear it, Will. But that's not why I asked you to step out here."

The Browns stood side by side in the shadows. I could feel them looking at me. Suddenly the night felt colder. I put my hands in my pockets. "What is it?" I asked. "What's wrong?"

"The company office was broken into tonight. Some important papers were taken. We know your grandfather took them."

CHAPTER 6
THE BREAK-IN

I couldn't believe my ears. Grandpa? *Stealing?* No way—not Old Charlie.

"Are you saying my grandfather just walked into your office and took your papers?"

"A window was broken."

"Why would an old man climb through a broken window to steal some papers he knows nothing about?"

Adler looked toward the Brown brothers. "Pete here saw him. He'll tell you."

Pete Brown stepped out of the shadows. "I'm sorry, Mr. Croft. But I saw him. He was walking away from the office with something under his arm."

"But you didn't see him steal anything?"

Adler said, "My office is a mile from here, over by the bridge. Charlie had no reason to be there."

"Is that so?"

The Break-in 33

"It was after dark, and the job had shut down for the day. My office was closed. Pete here was making the last of his rounds. That's when he saw the broken glass . . . and Charlie."

I was sure we didn't have the whole story. "Why don't you ask Grandpa why he was out there?"

"I was hoping you'd find out for me."

"This is your problem, Mr. Adler. I'll have no part of it."

He turned away and looked out toward the yard. "Not even to help Old Charlie?"

Adler had me and he knew it.

"All right," I said. "Tell me what you want me to do."

"Find those papers. While you're moving your grandfather, go through his things. If I get the papers back, I'll forget Charlie took them."

"What are they?"

"They're bills from companies we need to pay." Adler ran his fingers through his hair. "Look, Will. My job is on the line. First someone sets fire to the Hanson house. Then sugar ruins one of our tractors. Ghosts keep popping up along the river. And now my office has been broken into. How can I build a lake with all

34 *Trouble at Catskill Creek*

this going on? Charlie's got to be stopped, Will."

"I'll do what I can."

"Get me those papers."

I went back inside. Young Charlie was awake. Grandpa was holding him and whispering funny sounds into his tiny ears.

Karen came toward me. "What's wrong, Will? What did they say to you?"

"They think Charlie broke into Adler's office and took some papers."

Grandpa looked up. "Have a seat. I've got to hear this."

I told them everything. Grandpa smiled and played with the baby.

"Don't you care?" I nearly shouted. "They might call the police. You could go to jail!"

"Do you think I took Adler's papers?"

"Of course not."

"Then stop worrying. Nothing's going to happen."

I wished I could be so sure. "Did you go out tonight?" I asked.

"Yes, I did. I went for a walk."

"Did Pete Brown see you?"

"How should I know? He might have. I was minding my own business."

Karen said, "Charlie, what were you carrying under your arm?"

He played with the baby and didn't answer. If we pressed him, he'd get up and go visit his geese. Suddenly he said, "Maybe Mark Brown knows something about the papers."

"*Mark* Brown? Why?"

"Because he lied. He told Adler he was watching me at the time their tractor was ruined. But Brown's jeep wasn't out front of here that night. No one saw me go for my walk."

"Why do you think he lied, Grandpa?"

"If you ask me, he was up to no good."

A hundred questions with no answers ran circles in my head. Karen put a blanket around the baby. "It's late," she said. "We really must be going. Tomorrow's moving day. We'll need an early start."

"I'll take some of your things tonight," I said to Grandpa.

The bedroom was jammed with boxes. They were stuffed with old shoes and pictures of people no one remembered. I'd have to sort everything after the move, when Grandpa wasn't looking. If Adler's papers were hidden somewhere, it could take a while to find them.

I loaded up the backseat of the car. Karen and Young Charlie got settled in front. I started the engine and turned on the heat. Then I went to say good-bye to Grandpa.

The fire had burned itself out. Grandpa wasn't in the room. I went to the kitchen and found him gazing out the window.

"Grandpa?"

He turned around, surprised. He was hiding something behind his back.

"What's that?"

"Nothing, Will. Thanks for coming. It's good of you to help me. I'll see you tomorrow."

The Break-in 37

I saw it then, hanging to the floor. Grandpa was holding the long piece of leather I'd found in the tool house.

There was nothing for me to do but play his game. Pulling secrets out of Grandpa was harder than taking spots off a dog.

The car was nice and warm when I climbed inside. The baby was asleep in his little car seat. Karen asked, "Did Charlie break into Adler's office?"

"Grandpa isn't the stealing kind. He wouldn't climb through a broken window, even if he could. He wouldn't take what wasn't his and then walk off into the night."

"He does do strange things at times."

I turned the car toward Dutch Center. We drove up out of the valley along Catskill Creek. The light of a new moon was shining down on its rushing water and wet rocks.

Karen cried out.

"What is it?" I asked, slowing down.

She pointed toward the river. I carefully stopped the car so the baby wouldn't wake up.

Something large and white was moving along the banks of Catskill Creek.

CHAPTER 7
MOVING DAY

We couldn't see it clearly. "Stay here!" I whispered as I jumped from the car.

It was hard to run across the rocky ground. I fell once and cut my hand. When at last I reached the water, it was gone.

"Maybe it was moonlight hitting a rock," Karen said as we drove off. We both knew it wasn't.

"At least Grandpa can't be the ghost. He didn't have time to get here from his house."

"Are you saying you think the ghost is *real*?" Karen asked. "I liked it better when you thought it might be Charlie."

"It doesn't matter anymore. Tomorrow we'll move Grandpa to the new house. The day after that we'll move the geese."

Karen laughed softly. "That should be fun. How do you plan to move a lot of angry birds?"

Moving Day 39

I didn't know. "Rip says he'll help. We can use his pickup. I'll round up some of the cousins, too."

"I wouldn't miss that for the world."

The next morning, I left the house early and drove to Adler's office. It was a small building sitting on a hill above the lake bed. Close by was one end of the half-finished bridge. The office had been brought in on a truck. When the lake project was done, it would be trucked to another job.

The broken window was covered with a board. It was too high off the ground for Grandpa to climb through. In the sandy ground under the window were footprints and pieces of glass. I knocked on the door before stepping inside.

Two women were busy filing. They stopped to look at me when I walked in.

"Is Mr. Adler here?" I asked.

One woman shook her head. The other said, "I'm sorry. He's making his rounds right now."

"What about his wife?"

"I'm afraid Mrs. Adler never visits the valley. She doesn't care much for all the . . . dirt."

I went back outside and got in the truck. I hadn't come there to find Mr. Adler. I knew he'd be out checking on his workers. He did that every morning. But I'd wanted to see his office.

Adler's window had been broken from within. That's why there was glass on the ground outside. And the footprints I'd seen surely weren't Charlie's.

I followed a dusty road that ran down the hill and turned under the bridge. As I crossed the lake bed I could see Grandpa's house. It stood by itself next to the river.

I could hear saws from far off. Most of the trees in the valley were gone now. It was hard to believe this had once all been forest.

I found Grandpa in back of his house feeding the geese. He smiled at them as they grabbed at the corn. Moving the birds would be hard work. But they were an important part of Grandpa's life. I hoped the geese would enjoy the pond. I hoped Grandpa would think of the new house as his home.

I brought empty boxes from the car to the kitchen. As always, Grandpa had washed and put away his dishes. I pulled them from the cupboards and carefully packed them.

Karen came by later with Rip. Grandpa finally started helping us. Nobody talked very much. Our job was a sad one, yet it had to be done.

We made a lot of trips from Grandpa's old house to the new one. Most of the boxes were stored in the new garage. The new house was too small to hold them. At last the old house was empty. Charlie and I stood alone in front of its cold fireplace.

"I'm sorry, Grandpa."

"We couldn't stop them, Will."

"Karen and I are glad to have you next door. You'll get to see Young Charlie every day."

He smiled then.

"And you'll have your geese. Rip built a big pond for them."

"Thank you."

"It's time to go, Grandpa."

He looked at me sadly. "Not yet, Will. Please. I'd like to stay with my geese tonight. I'll sleep on the floor here in front of the fireplace."

I tried, really tried, to talk Grandpa out of it. He wouldn't change his mind. I drove home to get him a cot and blankets.

I offered to stay with him, but Grandpa wouldn't let me. "Go to your wife and baby. They need you. I don't."

Rip's truck was in our driveway. He was helping Karen cook dinner.

"Rip has a great idea," she said as I set the table. "Instead of waiting until tomorrow, why not get the geese tonight? They can't see very well in the dark. They'll be like sitting ducks, or almost."

"Are you sure, Rip? Will that work?"

Rip didn't really know. "If it doesn't work, we can go back tomorrow," he said.

I was dead tired. I'd rather have gone to bed than fight with geese all night. But it would be good to have the job done. And Rip's plan sounded like a smart one.

"I'll leave Goldy here," Rip said. "He's happy in anyone's kitchen."

The collie, sleeping in the corner, heard his name. He waved his tail without opening his eyes.

Rip and I dug up leather gloves, cloth bags, and flashlights. I telephoned around, and four cousins said they'd meet us in the valley.

"We're coming with you," Karen said as we got in the truck. She held the sleeping baby in her arms.

We didn't pass any other cars on Acorn Road. Karen said, "It's so dead now. I feel like we're the last people on earth."

"They'll be building a new road around the lake," I said.

Karen touched Young Charlie's soft face. "One of these days, it will all be over. No more trucks, no more noise."

"Just a lot of tourists," Rip said.

We pulled up to Grandpa's back gate. I walked around to the front door and went inside without knocking. Empty now, the house didn't seem like a home anymore.

"Grandpa?" I called. There was no answer. He must have gone out on one of his walks. I joined the others.

"Let's get to work," Rip said. "Old Charlie will be back soon. He can't be far off."

My cousins came then. They were ready for a good time. I laid out a plan of attack. "We'll have to be fast and careful. Put your gloves on. Get a bag over a goose's head, and then wrap your arm around its middle. Stay away from the claws or they'll tear you up. Put the geese in the back of your trucks. The covers are in place, so they'll be trapped inside."

Rip told them that the geese couldn't fly well. "But they'll sure try to. Their wings will hit you in the face if you don't do it right."

"Remember those claws," I said.

One cousin said we should leave the geese where they were. "When the lake fills with water, the birds will float to the top."

Rip laughed. "Old Charlie wouldn't float. And he's not about to leave his feathery family."

We stepped quietly along the path to the back of the house. The geese were sleeping in groups all over the yard. They looked like large silver bumps in the moonlight.

We learned at once that geese sleep very lightly. Maybe they couldn't see too well in the dark, but their ears worked just fine. Each goose held up its long neck and honked as loudly as it could.

Karen was sitting with the baby on the back steps of the house. I could see her laughing, but all I heard were geese.

"Circle them!" I shouted. I moved down toward Catskill Creek. If the birds got to the river, we'd never catch them. "*Now*, everyone. *Go!*"

The geese honked and ran together as we closed in on them. I held out a cloth bag and picked a goose to catch. It faced me, raised its wings, and hissed.

Suddenly the night blew apart with the sound of breaking glass. Yellow flames rose into the sky. For one long second, the world stopped. Then a new sound cut in above the cries of the geese. Karen was screaming.

CHAPTER 8
FIRE!

I was locked in wave after wave of shadow and sound. I could hardly move. Geese rushed around me, over me, under me, on their way to the river. Behind them, fire raced through my grandfather's house.

It was just like my dream. Only this time I saw frightened geese, not dancing ghosts.

"Karen!" I couldn't hear my own voice. *"Karen!"*

Someone grabbed my arm. It was Rip. He pulled me away, shouting in my ear as he did so. He pointed toward his truck. "I got them. They're safe!"

We reached the pickup and climbed up beside Karen and the baby. The other trucks had been moved away from the house. Rip drove out to the road and parked.

I shined the flashlight on Karen's white face. "You're bleeding!"

"It's nothing, really. Just some flying glass. I feel silly, screaming like that. But the baby's all right." Young Charlie looked up at us with wide blue eyes. Then he opened his little mouth and cried.

"Has anyone seen Grandpa?" I asked.

"Not yet. If he went for a walk, he'll see the fire for sure."

Karen asked, "Shouldn't we go to Dutch Center for help?"

Rip shook his head. "The flames can be seen for miles. The fire fighters are probably on their way here now."

"Let's find Grandpa," I said.

Karen stayed in the truck with Young Charlie. Rip and I walked around the fire. The bright flames hurt our eyes.

"Look at the geese!" Rip cried.

The fire may have scared them, but the birds didn't go far. Most of them had stopped honking. They'd pushed together into one big group. Their long necks waved above their fat bodies as they eyed the fire.

Ten minutes later the first truck came. Its loud horn set the geese off honking and running again.

At the same time, jeeps came out of the dark. Mr. Adler and his workers, dressed in street clothes, tried to help. It was too late. The house fell in on itself with a crash.

"It's just as well," I heard someone say. "There'll be less for us to plow under."

Then I saw Grandpa. He was standing by himself on the other side of Acorn Road.

Fire! 49

As I crossed the road I caught Grandpa wiping his eyes. I came up and put my arm around him.

Suddenly I saw a flash of lights out on the lake bed. "What was that?" I asked Grandpa. When he turned to look, the lights had gone out.

I borrowed a pickup and headed away from the river. An open window let in freezing wind. My headlights showed something moving out there. As I got closer, I saw a green jeep driving away across the valley floor.

I followed as fast as the pickup would go. The rocky ground nearly jarred me out of my seat. There were no trees there, and no place for the jeep to hide.

Straight ahead, up on a hillside, was Adler's office. To reach the road going uphill, the jeep had to turn under the bridge.

"Where are you going?" I cried when it missed the turn. I pushed the horn again and again. "You won't make it!" I slammed on my brakes just as the jeep's front tires hit the face of the hill.

The jeep went straight up and then flipped back over.

I jumped out of the pickup and ran to the jeep. I tried pulling on the driver's door. It wouldn't open.

"Hold on," I called out. I raced back to the truck to get some tools.

Lights came toward me from across the lake bed. A minute later Robert Adler was standing beside the jeep.

"The driver's trapped," I told him.

Adler took a short knife from his pocket. With great care, he cut a large hole in the jeep's cloth door.

I stood nearby, ready to help. Adler reached into the hole, speaking softly to the driver.

Rip raced up in his pickup. "What happened?" he asked. "Who's in there?"

I didn't answer right away. I now knew who had run from me. And I was pretty sure I knew who'd set fire to Grandpa's house.

"Give us a hand," I said. Together we gently pulled Darlene Adler out of the jeep.

CHAPTER **9**
ANSWERS AT LAST

We made a sorry-looking group around the kitchen table—Grandpa, Rip, Karen, and me. Our faces were still dirty from the fire. We needed rest, but no one felt like sleeping.

"Here you go," I said, dishing up eggs and bacon. "A late night breakfast."

Karen said to Grandpa, "I'm so sad about your house."

"We can be glad it was empty," I said. "Think what might have happened if anyone was inside."

"And the geese weren't hurt," Rip added.

Grandpa smiled at me. "Rip told me how you were going to round up my birds tonight."

"We'll get them tomorrow," I said.

Goldy was sleeping in the corner. I laid a piece of bacon on the floor in front of him. He opened his eyes, ate the bacon, and came looking for more.

"I hope Darlene will be all right," said Karen. "She's not really a bad person."

"No, she's not bad," I said. "Just weak. She couldn't control herself. Hate can be a strong power."

"Who does she hate?" asked Grandpa. "Her husband?"

"No, not Adler. She hates the mountains."

Grandpa didn't believe me. "Who could hate the Catskills?" Then he smiled. "Don't answer that, Will. I remember the things your father said before he left for New York."

Rip poured himself a glass of milk. "If everyone loved the mountains, New York City would move here."

Karen turned to me. "What else did Mr. Adler tell you tonight?"

I stopped to think. Adler had seemed to need a friendly ear while he waited in Doctor Master's office. I stayed to keep him company. The doctor was getting Darlene ready to go to a hospital in Albany. Her arm was broken, and she'd hurt her head.

"She'll be fine," the doctor told us. "But she hit her head pretty hard. I want to have more tests run."

So I'd waited with Adler, and finally gotten some answers.

"Darlene is like my parents," I said. "She loves the big city. All her friends are down in New York. All the big stores are there. And Darlene hates bugs, little animals, and plants that make your skin break out. She was going crazy up here. It got to the point where she just couldn't stand it anymore."

Karen smiled. "Darlene wasn't cut out for life in the country."

"Well," I said, "she finally got so bent out of shape she set fire to the Hanson house. She simply had to get out of here. She knew her husband was about to move them from Snowfall to Dutch Center. But living there wouldn't be much better. She wanted to go back to New York. With Adler."

"I think I get it," Rip said. "She was trying to make her husband look bad to his company. She wanted him to get fired. Then he'd have to go back to New York and look for another job. I'd guess she was the one who put the sugar in the gas tank, too."

"I thought Mark did it," said Grandpa. "After all, he lied about watching me that night."

"He had to," Karen told him, "or he'd get himself in hot water." She said to me, "I talked with the Brown brothers tonight while you were running around the valley. Mark was supposed to watch Grandpa that night. Instead he went to see his girlfriend."

I went on. "The fire at the Hansons' and the broken tractor weren't enough to get Adler fired. So one night Darlene went to her husband's office. She let herself in with his key.

"The papers might have been sitting out. They seemed important, so Darlene took them. She broke a window to make it look like someone had forced his way in.

"The woman in Adler's office told me Darlene never went there. Yet I found the footprints her city shoes made in the sand outside."

Grandpa laughed. "And people think *I'm* crazy!"

"Darlene wanted them to," I said. "She hoped people would believe you'd gotten so angry nothing mattered to you anymore. But that's where she went wrong. Even Adler knew you wouldn't burn down your own house."

"She went to a lot of trouble just to get back home," Grandpa said.

Answers at Last   55

Rip laughed. "You should talk."

Karen said, "Charlie, you once said even a mouse might bite if you took away its home. Maybe that's what Darlene did, only she went too far."

Rip sat down again. "What about the ghosts, Will? How did she do that?"

I looked straight at Grandpa. "She didn't," I said. "That was someone else's work."

"Charlie!" cried Karen. "You didn't!"

Grandpa looked away. "I never haunted the valley."

Grandpa was playing games. I said, "You took walks at night when no one was looking."

"So I like the cool night air."

"And do your geese feel the same way about it?" Charlie's old grin came back. "Tell me, Grandpa. Is there such a thing as a goose leash? Made of leather, perhaps? With three holes—one for the neck, and one for each wing?"

"There might be."

"And could a person then take a goose for a walk?"

"Maybe."

"And what would happen if the leash was pulled a little too hard?"

"The goose would open its wings and jump around. It tries not to fall down."

Rip and Karen were laughing. I didn't think it was so funny. "And what happens if you bring a second goose?"

Grandpa was clearly having a good time. He pulled out his pipe. "It will follow the first one."

Rip slapped the table. "So there weren't any ghosts—just big white birds. That's too bad. The ghosts make for a better story."

"It's not all fun, you know. Sometimes a goose gets off the leash. Then I have to spend half the night trying to get it home. Some of my birds are still out there."

"Then it was a goose we saw by Catskill Creek," Karen said. "One that got away."

"And that's why Grandpa was at Adler's office when Pete saw him," I said. "He was looking for a goose."

Old Charlie nodded. "George doesn't like the leash much. I couldn't find him by the river, so I walked over toward the bridge."

"Carrying the leash?" Rip asked.

"Right."

Karen stood up and cleared the table.

"It's time for me to go," said Rip. "What a day." I said good-bye, and Karen walked him to the front door.

Grandpa put his pipe away. "You can sleep here tonight," I said to him. "Tomorrow we'll set you up in the new house. Karen and I will do everything we can to make you happy."

A smile crossed his tired face. "Don't worry too much, Will."

"I think you'll be fine."

"We'll see," he said.

CHAPTER **10**
CROFT LAKE

Karen and I were standing on Grandpa's wide front porch. The whole valley was laid out before us.

"It's such a beautiful lake," Karen said. "I never thought it could be so nice."

"It almost looks like it's always been there," I said.

The door opened behind us, followed by the sound of little feet. I picked up Young Charlie. "See the pretty lake?"

He pointed down the hill. "Goose Lake!"

"That's *Croft* Lake," I said, then laughed. Only tourists used the right name.

Grandpa joined us on the porch. "Goose Lake fits it better, Will. You remember it took you three days to catch all my birds. Without Goldy's help, you and Rip would still be out looking for them."

"We should have thought of using Goldy right away," I said. "Collies are good at herding."

"Heads up," Karen said. "Look who's here."

Young Charlie waved as Robert Adler walked up the hill. He stopped at the bottom of the steps. "I've come to say good-bye. My job here is done."

"Have a seat on the swing," said Grandpa.

He shook his head. "Thanks, Charlie, but I have to leave in an hour. It's time to go home to New York. My wife and a new project are waiting for me there."

Karen said, "Darlene will be glad to have you back."

"Yes," said Adler, "she will. Now I can spend all my time there, not just weekends, like I've been doing."

"You know, she's a new person now," he went on. "She's been seeing a doctor every week. She's been working very hard to put her life in order."

Adler frowned. "I should have listened to her before. She was so unhappy here. But she didn't want to hurt anyone. Your house was empty, Charlie. She knew my company owned it and that we were tearing it down. She thought you'd already moved out."

Grandpa walked down the steps and held out his hand. "We know all that, son. But you've got to let the past be past. Look ahead."

I smiled to hear Grandpa say that. He'd changed a lot since moving up the mountain. He'd put in a garden and was taking care of even more geese. And he now had another Croft to listen to his stories.

Karen brought out a bottle of wine.

"Let's make a toast," I said after she'd poured it.

We touched glasses and held them out toward the lake.

"To even better tomorrows," Grandpa said. "May we have many of them."